AF802690

Words Like These

Words Like These

Bruce Wetteroth

An Ohio Review Book
Athens, Ohio

Copyright 1986 by Bruce Wetteroth
Published by Ohio Review Books, Athens, Ohio 45701–2979
All rights reserved.
Several of these poems have previously appeared in magazines as follows: in The Ohio Review, "Rig Song", "Seeing by Night", "Night of the Lyrids", "On a Bright Windy Day in Nebraska", "Tansy at Dachau", and "Moving on in November"; in *Poetry Now,* "Getting Lost"; in *Poetry Northwest,* "Just After"; in *Bitterroot,* "Wilderness"; in *The Nebraska Review,* "Salvage"; in *The American Poetry Review,* "Watching the Dancers from Peking".
Also several poems appeared in the chapbook "Life in Progress," published by The Ohio Review.

Library of Congress Cataloging in Publication Data
Wetteroth, Bruce
Words Like These.

(An Ohio Review Book)

I. Title.

PS 3573.E927W67 1986 811′.54 86–23523

ISBN 0–942148–07–X
ISBN 0–942148–06–1 (pbk.)

Composition by Chappel Typesetting, Athens, Ohio
Manufactured in the U.S.A.
Publication of this book has been aided by a grant from the Ohio Arts Council.

CONTENTS

III

I

Moving On In November

Failed again in the
doing nothing while my wife worked,
I drove to the lake.

The road goes right down in the water
as if there still could be a road
down there, coming up in oozy vegetation.

My coffee steamed the windshield
and I was waiting
as if for an invisible boatman,
skimming the surface in a patch of wind.

A few boats lay there upside down,
the water lapping their sterns.
There was one leaf flapping on the sycamore.

It was a day I could imagine my mother
at the piano, playing Brahms. It's from her
I have my liking for these
loose ends of the year,

a solemn orchestration in the oaks
across the lake. Dense
harmonies, like smoke.

I watched cloud shadows as they climbed the hill,
dropping out of sight in the next hollow,
while the shadow of the shadows went on rising.

Night of the Lyrids

I've walked almost beyond the ring
of a hundred watt bulb above the cabin door.

I've walked off far enough to quiet the dog
who knows I've stopped being part of the music.

Still, I can't walk far enough not to hear it—
a band of professors, gathered with guitars,
making a gentle bluegrass under the glow
of kerosene lamps and warmed by a Franklin stove,
with bread and cheese spread on a wooden table.

All at once it reminded me of riding the boat
at King's Island through a gallery
of scenes from Walt Disney and Mother Goose
to a bouncy tune that kept coming back
with renewed emphasis from hidden speakers,
echoing all that's wholesome in America,
enriched cereals, icicles dripping at the eaves—

you step from the boat to a revolving platform,
one of the worlds still spinning, you're not sure which.
Then months later you find yourself in a supermarket,
trying to do that tune with soft, popping sounds at your lips.

So I've stepped out here to smoke and test my soul
against the constellations, which are hard tonight.
Leo, for example. Never much of a lion.
It has no head, for one thing, and it prances.
Virgo, never much of a constellation.
I think I could reorganize the sky

with two stars from Virgo and two from Berenice's Hair
and make something simpler: the Straight Line.

A meteor comes burning out of the west,
a vanishing incision, like a seam
opening in the ecliptic and sealing again.
Along the way it x's out my line
then flares out like a match somewhere past Hydra.

So where are we, this night of the Lyrids?
Ten miles west of a university town
with a few white lights and red radio tower,
worried by the dog, hoping he'll let us back in,
learning the stars, like anything else,
learning to share an illusion.

Rig Song

It rose one day from a weedy lot
between townhomes and condominiums
like the tower of an antique battleship
battling the flatlands. I'd swear
it had not been there in the morning.

*

It raised red lights above the tennis courts,
pointing more or less toward Rigel
the way things point at stars,
approximately and out of scale,
like the donor in a late medieval painting,
pointing faintly in the general direction
of the saints or the Mother of God.

*

After a week or two it began to sing:
a little like the cry of the snow goose
skipping across the night;
or more like the song of the humpback whale,
carrying halfway across the Pacific,
singing not quite by our human scale,
with odd harmonics that are nature's alone,
but ringing with a quality of sound
Mozart could have mastered and composed for,
increasingly melodious with distance.

*

It sang in the most difficult direction,
to tap the richer dark a half mile down.
It sang straight down into the dragon's blood
that may or may not be there underfoot.
And so its singing rose like half a guess
and woke me for some nights. Like a tuning fork
touched with the troubled musics of the earth
and buried treasures. It sang like anyone
for love or money. It sang with shrieks of steel
and howling overtones, a little out of control.

Views of Alicia

For a day or two it's nothing personal,
a shapeless animal,
sprawled across the Gulf of Mexico.
Then its eye starts narrowing
as it wanders in our direction.

It has become a new kind of weather,
a dry gusting that accelerates all morning.
Then a free ride home in the afternoon.
We stop along the way to strip the markets
of bread and candles. We notice windows
x'd with tape as for a Passover.
It's becoming twice as much weather as we've seen,
twice as much warning as we've had about anything.
Looking up, it is a view from below
of the satellite pictures, the turning edge
of a giant carousel, striped with cloud and a perfect blue,
a blue coming in all the way from the Caribbean.

*

By night, pure fury: piques of wind
like a catfight on the windowsill.
A whistling blade that stops an inch short
of the glass. A revision of Tao, a violent wind
that will not blow over by morning,
ringed with tornados like Grecian curls
in a light disorder, a wind without instinct—
trees have surrendered but it won't let them up.
A trashcan crosses the parking lot in a single bound.
The rain is horizontal, misting the room through a crack.

All at once it has become highly personal,
as when it blows your radio station right off the air.

*

And why is there something almost consoling
in its vowels, as if it were full
of something that was missing from our lives?
All night it never tires of I-told-you-so's.
I told you you were living a dream.
I told you your roofs were temporary.
Your cars, your beachfront properties, all your utilities.
And there are people who can sleep through this?
They need to be told. It's full of everything
I was trying to tell you. Or I think I was trying.
Or I don't know. I'll try again in the morning.

Least Bittern

The least bittern is trying to freeze
in mid-air between two cattails,
one in each foot and a wind rising.

It's just across the ditch at a range
where field glasses begin to curl your vision
inward, into the dimension of presbyopia.

But there's all the time in the world to note
red lores, yellow eyes,
all the creamy buff and black markings,

the long nose like Pinnochio's,
the comic aspect of heronry in general,
especially in a heron the size of a meadowlark.

I sit there while the cooling fan
clicks off in my engine.
I look away and think of other things.

I'm sure there were eyes and minds wandering
all over Golgotha the day of the crucifixion.
Mine wander farther down this sideroad in Texas

then finally back to this great little bird
I might not see for another fifty years.
The least bittern has remained frozen

not much better than I've been watching,
though surely both of us are doing better
than some of the guests at Cana—

sopping up the wine,
only vaguely suspecting a miracle,
amazement fading, if not the honor of the occasion.

Unanswered Question

I asked the wind, are you there?
A leaf tumbled into the house.

The wind is thieves, or a madman
wandering in from the street
with silvery eyes like dimes.

It's you gone blind.
Or coming home too early
with an amnesia
stringing before your eyes
like a spiderweb.

Seeing in the Dark

There's something that works with its teeth
in our bedroom wall.

It's there whenever I start
dropping off.

I rap. It looks up in the dark.

It runs. It runs across the ceiling,
little feet tapping like the fingertips
of a Paderewski, drumming arpeggios on a dummy keyboard.

I doze.
It gets back to work,
I see a kind of white
static in its teeth.
I look up in the dark.

Waiting Outside the Nature Center

The snake came sliding like water uphill
out of the garden pond in the Arboretum.
It held a minnow sideways in its mouth
and kept one eye on me as it swallowed it.

Re-entering the water from a narrowing rock ledge,
it left barely a ripple until the tail
dropped in with a light plop.
It vanished from the surface without a trace.

Then I spotted its head,
resting there like a twig. The body
pulsed below, a few dark lines
slightly more vivid than the rest of the water.

Then a Brownie Troop came crowding around.
I said
it might come up sooner if you gave it more room.
They stepped back, but still it did not come up.

You start to wonder what you are looking for.
It seemed one of the purer forms of awareness:
whatever a garter snake can keep of you
in one red eye while swallowing a minnow

or hold below, waiting for you
not to be there.
Something
for which a simple description would suffice.

Dirigible

The last time I saw the Goodyear Blimp
there were two of them,
tipping their noses into a headwind,
up, down, sideways,
like a team of horses, happily.

This evening there was only one,
hung like a whale above Greenway Plaza,
circling the city in search of its lost mate.

*

How I love the pathetic fallacy. It is my favorite.
But I don't dare say it. I feel
how seriously I'm ceasing to amuse you
as we sit there side by side
almost like strangers on the Westheimer bus.

*

I like the way a dirigible
seems to be getting nowhere over the years,
so that even a bus will gradually
overtake it through the evening traffic.
And the way it turns,
as if a whole team had to get out
and help direct it around a corner,
as if any maneuver were delicate,
as if it didn't have all the room in the world
to make a turn in.

*

So I don't know what to tell you. Certainly
none of these lighter-than-air associations,
nor the thing I heard that pleased me once—
how easy it was to steer the Goodyear Blimp.

You're not even watching it.
You're not even thinking
how much happier we were
so few Superbowls ago.

Cleaning Up the Leftover Words

For some years now the words have been
our particular problem. We've abandoned
a ton of them since West Virginia.

And now this life ended but the apartment
full of books.

All those words first read in better days
make no engaging sense now. Reading on
becomes a duty, like doing dishes,
pushing maybe to the end of a chapter.

You can keep all the fiction. I'm not planning
to leave a word of poetry in the place.

Not even my last word of belated
connection, tying the telephone to the bolted door.

Maybe I'll be sorry for what I said,
but how can I be sorry for thinking it?

Funny, all these things I'll not be telling you.
Isn't there anything more I'll be telling you?

Only that I never meant for it
to end like this
in debt and silence.

Route

Left off Pech and curving to the right
down Leafy Lane around three a.m.—

Ah Leafy Lane, you've come back like a dream
in the middle of the afternoon.
                                                            I see
how much I'm starting to love that part-time work
but secret profession at three a.m.
where I can stop. Go back. Correct my errors.

I love especially the part that begins
with a pole on the lawn down Leafy Lane
and the little horsehead shining in my lights,
where Leafy Lane starts curving into Krist,
which turns into Winningham,
and cul de sacs, and neighborhoods that become
increasingly labyrinthine at three a.m.
The empty streets are pure topology.
The houses stand like pictures in a cave.

Part of it is logic, Ariadne's thread
winding through the otherworld of that hour.
Much of it pure ear—listening
for the slap, satisfied
the *Times* has landed safely in a drive;
or the airy sound the car makes,
sailing through the stopsign on Leafy Lane.

Compared to which we sleepwalk through our days,
dreaming our way through traffic,
half the time not knowing where we are.

I doze and think I've dreamed you, Leafy Lane,
but you are real and moving the whole while
like the river I really saw once, underground.
You go on hollowing your place in me.
You're rising like a woman to every sense.
I love your gentle curve that seems to breathe.
I'll love you until the Key Map comes alive.

Your Name

It's not hard imagining what the woman felt
this afternoon, being helped from the ditch
where her Chevrolet was scraping its frame.

She felt as we might feel in a suddenly
darkened room, trying to catch our balance,
even without the blood in one eye.

We can feel what the old man felt
still pinned by gravity in the back seat,
lifting a hand to wave,
waving as though he should know us.

This is a hand,
he waved,
although for the moment
I seem to have forgotten whose.

*

So you know how I felt a little later
running into you at the supermarket.
I felt how lightly a proper name can sit
on us, like a paper cup
resting on the floor of a vehicle.

There between the aisles and the displays
of named things, I tried to talk my way
around your missing name,

certain it would come to me in a moment,

hopping into visibility
like a thrush on a woodland path.

It might have if you had not been so pretty.
That made the talk seem wild
and almost too intimate in the sense of everything

you were not. We'd never
traveled anywhere together.
We'd never even slept in the same house.
You were not my sister. Not my wife.

On a Bright Windy Day in Nebraska

We're sitting on the patio with Aunt Lill
who can still say things about the weather.
She sees the wind and the dark red flowers.
Her seeing comes and goes. It is not in her eyes.

"Eva should be here by now," she says.
"Eva won't be here," says Betty this morning.
(Eva's dead, Jean said. She's been dead five years.
Oh? Lill said. That makes me sad to hear it.)

"Well it's been nice but we'll have to be going.
Eva will be coming to take me home."
"You are home," Betty says. "This is your house."
"I don't understand what's keeping Eva so long."

"We'll see her later," I say. Betty looks at me.
"We used to have a dog named Nissie," Lill says,
"but I think he's gone. So I think I won't call him."
(Nissie? Jean explained. That was eighty years ago.)

Lill winces and winces, her eyes milking the light.
"Look at all those red flowers up there on the bank."
"Roses," I raise my voice and say. "Those are the Olson's roses."
"There are three women," she says, "sewing up there in the dark."

Carter Lake

There are cormorants raising their chests
and beating their wings all over Carter Lake.

It takes a while for them to fly. They have to run
a little ways across the water.
When they get off it's OK.
They fly well enough in a straight line.

The cottonwood by the water is flapping, too,
louder and louder with October.
It's a huge tree. It's not
going anywhere.

The bottomlands are wide, the river lost
between the bluffs, sleeping in Carter Lake.

The trees that try to line the river
are totally confused by now
about which side is Iowa and which Nebraska.

The cottonwood doesn't know but I was born here,
if this is Nebraska. I've defended it over the years,
notably against my eighth-grade teacher who said
there were no trees in Nebraska. Even though
I ended up sitting outside the principal's office

raising my chest and beating my wings.

II

Paths Around the Lake

A coot patters out underfoot
loudly and in great agitation.
We're breathing hard, wearing out the body,
pretending we can't remember which God
so loved the world He
dropped these yellow bows through the low ground,
scattered handkerchiefs up the hillside,
breathed a red frost into the redbud.

*

We swing along the lake trail waving
at the Sunday fishermen. Some of them stare.
There may not be as many of us
as sometimes we think: augurs, auspices,
walkers swinging a PanAm bag
from shoulder to shoulder,
full of tools for naming things.
Why should they see what I see,
Samuel Constantine Rafinesque
dancing after Audubon and me,
wanting to hug us both at each new flower?
Look too hard and we all vanish
like a hologram seen from the wrong angle.

*

I swing along and stop dead when I see the veery.

The way the thrushes move,
off to a low branch facing away.
The second time they move they're gone forever.

A Small Cry

On the first warm day in March
I almost stepped on a prodigy:
a garter snake with two front legs
and a tiny voice, a nasal wailing
so far away that my first thought
was someone was making fun of me.

But it was calling distinctly: help.

I changed sex. I knew the future.
I saw two things clairvoyantly:

first that I would not stay around
for the denouement, frog feet
slipping like hands from a window ledge,
leaving a quiet lump in a long throat.

Second that this could not be
a general condition, this walking
through the woods with binocular vision
and a sense of something larger than
ourselves engulfing us from behind.

It would not even make sense
in the universe unless there were
other planets where we were all
warmblooded, and ate grass.

But here we are as peculiar
to the time and place as a
giant headdress of quetzal feathers;

or an Aztec dancer, looking out
from the mouth of a jaguar.

Clearing Away a Doubt

The cicada sounds like someone
who means to line out everything,
covering the noon with a coil that goes on
and on like an exercise in penmanship,
right down to the stub of an indelible pencil,
down to the bare intention and still scraping furiously,
turning the day the color of zinc or pewter.

There was never a demonstrable need
for any of this: stars or habitable planets,
or what we call singing, struck up again
the moment the clouds come over at noon.
Except when it stops the quiet is ionized.
It's cleansed the ear like a scouring brush
and left a taste of scouring powder in the air.
The light is chastised with raw relief. But
that's the only need for any of this at all.

Looking Up at Noon

Bare feet moving in the house.
What are you doing? the boy will ask.
Nothing, I'll say, leave me alone.
Who was famous, he asked me once,
when you were alive?

There's a thunder, small in the distance.
The cricket has fallen silent at noon.
After all, they are only words,
they are only a courtesy,
a paradox, a nostalgia, an ambition,
a green light frozen on the mossy stone.

Sleep and Poetry

Sleep crawls up the windshield,
a transparent crab,
walking in time with the wipers.
I shake my head but he is everywhere,
waving a jeweled tail,
climbing over my eyelids,
prying at my head as though
it were a clam.
Something in him is incredibly ugly.
It is his beauty that makes him dangerous,
his suggestion that nothing is serious.

Keeping One's Distance

Down in the hollow someone is target-shooting:
a sound like a board
being hammered to the air in slow-motion.

Up here the grouse goes walking
like someone important, watching for an assassin.

A fly buzzing in the leaves
is a sound like voices: boys
whose voices are changing as they hurry closer.

Unhistorical Moment

Around dinner time, I look up.
Something is different.
For almost a minute no car
has passed up there on the highway

and the sun has stopped
low over the embankment
to lay a great hand on my forehead
like a bear's, restraining its power.

A minute or two like the long peaceful reign
of one of the Antonines
with no invasions, no conquests.

A field sparrow sings, clear in the distance.
Three times.
Each time more sweetly.

Making My Own Path

The trail ends under the pines.
It looks as though it might storm.
The storm is only sunlight
on the gray woods above.

Under the pines it is colder.
I find owl pellets
and the wing of a crow.

*

Wading through mayapple
along the level bank
where the spring beauty has laid
a white net on and on

my hat is snatched off.
A spider hangs from my glasses, pulling in.
The web on my face: a thought
of dying where no one knows me,
all these years old and still hating work.

Getting Lost

Follow any watercourse down
and you'll come to the Gulf of Mexico.
Getting lost is rather a frame of mind,
just as it was always a function of time,
something you work at in Southern Ohio,
an hour or two spent losing a trail
that vanishes into the white of the county map.

There may be a mastery of the art:
an illusion of being about to arrive
at a ridge where columbine survives
or a hollow where no one comes,
no sound of traffic, easier maybe
in the hills and in the rain.
Then stepping onto a familiar road
as though it were the Peach Blossom Kingdom.

Tomorrow in Parkersburg

A neighbor is hosing out some metal basin:
a rushed sound like a wind before rain,
quickly drowned as the tub starts filling.

It sounds like an old-fashioned washtub,
the kind we used to hose out in the backyard,
thirty years and five hundred miles away,
zinc-gray and lusterless
as the uniforms of the Saint Louis County Police.

A streetcar used to run all the way out
to Creve Coeur Lake. One of us said
somebody from New York would probably believe it
if we told them Indians might attack us
out of those woods along the way.
It rang true. People from New York are so dumb.

Some things come back and some are gone forever.
This may not be puzzling.

Tomorrow there will be a mystic
lecturing over in Parkersburg.
Stay in perfect health, she promises.
Answer any of the age-old questions.

Sycamore

In August the bark is lit
like a Dutch interior, filled
with a silence of milk
being poured in a deep tin.

Sunday morning. All at church.
Here the Lord goes on sleeping
while Spinoza has begun
grinding a lens upstairs.

The artist goes on discarding
scraps from his studio. The anarchist
is hard at work in the waters below,
uprooting a square of sidewalk.

On the Track of the Lady's Slipper

This hilltop has so much the look
of other ground where they have been,
shining with the same dry light
and lichen, silent after the rain,

I stoop beside a fallen pine
and think it is time to see one now,
hopped into being like a thrush, and only
something in my eyes that cannot find it.

Remembering Rosalind

Ah these misty September mornings—
as though you could take the trees by their shoulders
and slide them lightly here and there
over the bumpy ground.

Like dancing with the drunken girl, Rosalind,
shuffling and laughing across the wooden floor,
ripe as a melon going on nineteen,
her shoulders firm beneath her sweaters . . .

Morning: a marble rolling in your pocket,
a cricket in the coal cellar,
the earth tilting under your feet.

The earth has been going on four billion years.
But when were there ever days like these?

On a Rainy Day
I Remember Magna Mater

Another forty dollars on the van
and it still sounds like a tin can.

All our appliances, burned out one by one.
I was depressed for two days, trying to install a washing machine.

There is rainwater in our "high dry cellar,"
the seeping toes of Hurricane Frederick.

I see rain dripping the length of our raingutter,
slowed at the eaves, like a tantric discipline.

The rain is battering down the asters
and the great lobelia along the creek.

I count my blessings and discover ambiguities.
I put on Mozart's G minor piano quartet

and find even melancholy will not stay
in one place. Mixed feelings, as when the cat

went out for the first time in two years
and left a shrew, garnished in honeysuckle, on the doorstep.

It is the season to think of roots.
I think my roots are in the sea, the road.

Or with the swallows, gathering along wires,

quietly, nervously, unable to get on.

A sudden longing for the mountain flowers:
I want to find the gentian one last time.

A longing to transcend the world of matter
yet all the while be pleasing to Magna Mater,

a wild and mythical desire let it be said.

Alpine Memory

We carried a mirror between us
down the mountain all afternoon,
filling it with gentians and every
forget-me-not along the path.
It grew so full that when the dark
surprised us, we left it overturned,
spilling its light in the cool needles.

Leaving Another Life Behind

Their honor is a toad, a loaded pistol,
left in your desk without explanation,
a rope thrown over your doorsill.

I've planned my exitus: put shoes
on your head and back from their office
mumbling apologies in French or Latin.

Let them wake without a clear impression
of what was said, as the suicide awakens
not realizing at first whose wound it is.

Meanwhile the painful thing has been averted.
Down on the rainy street the cars are rushing
toward the dawn that will bury their headlights.

Life in Progress

This morning the sun walked into the house
like a blind man. I held my breath.
There was something so fragile in the room,
traced over the carpet from the window frame,
the rocking chair, like a shadowgraph
of some structure in a higher dimension
than I could envision or the cat suspect,
washing herself right in the middle of it.

Today I petted a skunk: a dry coarse wool;
a restlessness in the bony back;
an absence of mind as he nibbled my fingers,
then hurried to pry open a cabinet, being nocturnal.
The naturalist hauled him out for the next visitors.
I thought she too would rather be left alone.
I watched a ratsnake coiling on itself,
an exercise in perpetual motion; a turtle
sitting on a rock in its glass case
with blinking eyelids and a hostile expression,
captive animals like people stricken,
dazed by the light, crawling. . .

We drove from Burr Oak to McConnellsville,
a sleepy town on Sunday afternoon,
among those places we visit once
and then it is as if we had never been there,
back by way of Amesville to a houseful
of obligations: tax-forms treated
with an invisible explosive,
dangerous to handle if you have not first

sighed, and put the creatures in their places.
Making sense of things can be like an
assassination: no evidence will quiet every suspicion.

Media in vita

For a while no rain touched me.
Only a few drops came tumbling
like vireos through the lower leaves.
A toad the size of a walnut hopped
from the path and lay atop the grass
like a rubber toy, hoping it was not seen.
But I saw even the pulse of its heart,
striking now and then in its side
like a raindrop. And heard the drumming
of a grouse, that sound that comes
as if from your own body.

III

Wilderness

There is a wilderness that will preserve itself
in the squeal of starlings at twilight across a bridge
or the chirping of sparrows around a barn.
The things that Mozart reaches with a turn of phrase.
The things we forget to tell someone who dies.

Just After

When my sister called I think
this light snow was already falling
like a drive all night.

I pick up the Bible you never read
or questioned. He cometh forth
like a flower and is cut down.

I can't imagine you being impressed
I opened right there.

I pick up the Zen paperback you never read
or heard of: Hokei, the Happy Chinaman,
being asked what is the actualization of Zen,
swung his sack over his shoulder
and went his way.

His sons
come to honor and he knoweth it not.
Et cetera.

Tomorrow we'll be driving through the night.
For now I have a few hours
alone with your death.

I'll watch this snow like a journey
already begun. A call to prayer.
A trainride years ago.

And still I'll barely have a coat and tie
and only words like these.

I'll stop what I was doing.
I'll do the dishes.
I'll finally throw out the broken cup.

Salvage

We had our shots for tetanus but not against
the strangeness of the place,
wrenched in its frame and baptized in the flood.

The house was like a stranger
or someone changed
after a stroke,
or converted, born again,
remade of something tough—it took
three swings of the axe at one storm window
to let some air in.

I shoveled a path as far as the laundry room
and wheeled out muck into the yard.
Aunt Lu sifted through it like a judge:
jewelry and spoons into the water,
books to the fire, where they refused to die,
like shoes, or the thought of Uncle Paul.

I know there was a part of my uncle
that would have loved to see it, his house
up to its eaves in the Mississippi,
the film of yellow silt all through his garden,
the ghost hung ten feet up into the trees.

You're gone, you're gone, was his philosophy.
Yet I think he so would have enjoyed it
he hung around the house that afternoon,
confirmed in skepticism, its living proof.

He would have enjoyed seeing us grit our teeth

and try to accept the river's gifts: the frog
that hopped from a kitchen cabinet.
The snake Aunt Lu killed at the front door.
The shreds of memory all through the floodplain.

I liked the herons standing in a cornfield.
The gallinules swimming in front of the car.
The big rivercrab, wobbling across the road.

The lake half-drowned. The thought there were people
who got by with it. The retirement.
The easy fishing. The having lived there.

The Other Night

The other night when our friends were here
we showed our slides from the Smithsonian.
The kids kept walking in front of the screen:
T-shirts salted and speckled with light
and tinged with the glowing rust of nebulae.
Odd, as if the stars were shining through them.
They liked the feeling and kept coming back,
star-children, raising their hands to touch
the wound, to show how insubstantial. . .

Later the dead came, drawn to the Christmas lights
and their black reflection in the window.
I sat there late and magnified myself,
imagining they needed my eyes to see,
my mind to be there. I offered them
the firelight in my glass, and tried to imagine
what they had come to tell.
Hail and Farewell,
something like that, for what we need
is less the words than the assurance
that they would care to visit our world again.
Of course we'll never stop trying to bring them back,
although the closer they come the sharper our pain.

Watching the Dancers from Peking

When the princess comes to a river
to cross in a boat that is not a boat,
having no color and no substance,
nothing of a boat but the axes on which
it spins and dips and rolls out of control,
because the boatman is not a boatman
but a Chinese dancer on a stage,
and the river is not a river but a section of stage,
and the situation is comic with every motion
slowed to the rhythm of waters which are not waters

but something we have also seen
as if painted an inch above a canvas,
riding into our world through a weightless lens
which left us wanting to see like William Turner—

we also want to move like a Chinese dancer
in the lingering presence of those waters,
so real is the invisible and so great our need.

Getting the Job Done

I rest on my shovel, laureled with sweat.
There's someting restful in loose dirt,
tumbling down, seeking a level,
while our landlord goes on complaining.

Says he's worked
half his life around the oilfields
and never heard of fooling with a gasline
behind the meter.
Anything up to the meter is their responsibility.
Any fool knows that.
He's made two scenes at Columbia Gas
but you can't tell them anything.
Learns something new every day.

In these three days since the runaway truck
took out our line, he's come to seem
a great man. He looks like Truman.
Nearing eighty and not quite satisfied
even now, as the line lies buried.

Grudgingly, he nods down at the soil.
"This new stuff should last a hundred years,"
he says, "if nobody breaks it."

Growing Moccasins

Too sick for school in the morning,
by afternoon he was feeling fine.
We pulled on shoes and explored the ridge.

The deer track led into a trail
and took us over one of those knobs
with big trees, white oak, shagbark.

I guessed it was an Indian mound.
He was willing to believe it. Usually
on a hilltop overlooking a river.

Sure enough, a little farther on
we saw through trees
down onto the shopping mall,

Kroger's lettered there clean and small
and the river just behind.
It was a nice moment,

single leaves against the sunlight,
lamps left on in the woods,
yellow, carmine.

We'd found a secret passage to Kroger's
and had a choice—to go on
or melt back, unseen,

as if we could melt back like Shawnee
and no one in town would ever know

how close we had come to their lives.

I think he felt it, though we were very quiet.
I know I would have at thirteen.
I still did.

Auto Graveyard

All those Bonnevilles, Fords, and Datsuns, were once
loved and polished, equipped with options.

It took just seconds to jam their doors, pop open
their trunks, twist their bumpers like tags on a
trashbag. Each of those thick spiderwebs of crystal
was once a dream come to a screeching halt.

It's so sad about your Camaro—your first car, and
not your fault. Still, I can't help swearing at it.
I'm trying to work the speakers free of their mounting
in the trunk, skinning my knuckles on raw metal, while
cold crawls up my back.

One of the speakers is still alive. Its magnet won't
let me work the screwdriver calmly. There's a bolt I
end up ripping free like a mandrake root. But finally
I have the weight of it in my hands. I hold it care-
fully, as if I were Goethe lifting Schiller's skull.
It's full of something invisible that must not be
spilled. I'm afraid I'm spilling it. Though I don't
know why it matters, here, where things are spilled
and parts drop loose like bones in an ossuary. Here
where we learn the value of material things. Here
where the insurance ends.

Seeing by Night

The lightning bugs
are rising from the lawn.
By midnight they've risen
as high as the trees.
As they rise they flash. When they flash again
they're elsewhere, like stars,
the light just now reaching us.

*

For a while a barred owl hoots
from the maple across the street.
It sounds remoter. Space begins to close
around its hooting,
which takes time,
a thousand years to cross the street.
By the time it reaches us
the owl is gone, the voice
hung like a telephone in the tree.

*

Then the night cools. I dream
a hearse has come sailing into our driveway
with no sound but tires on gravel.
The driver stands with cap in hand,
apologizing for some change in plans.
He'd like to leave the casket now
and get on with his other deliveries.
Sometime soon the director should arrive
with the funeral party.

*

All day we miss the luminosity
in the mind, glowing like a watch dial.
Sometimes we only see it with closed eyes.
But when it comes, we also feel compassion
for these bodies, cast aside
like so much dirt. Certainly we need
these bodies, to become visible to one another.
Mother, Father, I'm thinking of you
more often than you'll imagine.
But would you want a letter like this?

Tansy at Dachau

It was a day of glaring omissions
under the pleasant Bavarian sun,
starting with the Chamber of Commerce sign,
the town that wanted to be remembered
for something else, we forget what.

Then the faces scratched from the historical
posters in the museum, yet could not be
scratched from memory. Gaps
in the statistics. People
liberated with religion: none.

Leaving the register unsigned,
we skipped the barracks and crematorium,
stopping only to have our snapshot taken
before the memorial of twisted steel
with dates in black like twelve years
missing from the light.

We struggled a little for an attitude
toward the children just arriving
in high spirits on their field-trip bus.
We were leaving by way of the gate
that still says: Work will free you.

It was the field of poppies
and lack of visible evil in the view
from the parking lot: trim white buildings
peaceful as an Army post in Kansas,
white gallows shaped like a work of art nouveau—

I got out the Instamatic once again
and noticed the tansy just inside the fence.

There were all the things we still didn't know
about this flower beyond its name
and bare identity. We hadn't learned
how in the 1400's its oils were kneaded
in Paschal cakes in memory of the bitter herbs.
We hadn't read about its reputation
as an abortive, persisting into this century,
nor how its acrid scent would keep
two centuries in a crypt. How it escaped
cultivation in New England to become an American
wildflower. All the things that gave us chills
reading them later in a book.
                                        We found
a flower without petals
persisting along a fence.
A tough and stunted flower
that brought fierce tears at once.

Bruce Wetteroth was born in Omaha and raised in Saint Louis, where he graduated from Washington University with degrees in Psychology and General Literature. He studied German Literature at the Johns Hopkins University and for some years taught German and Humanities at West Virginia State College. More recently he has lived in Mexico, Ohio, Texas, and Nebraska, studying, writing, working in a library, teaching English as a Second Language, and doing odd jobs. His chapbook, *Life in Progress*, was published in *The Ohio Review* in 1982. This is his first book-length collection of poems.